Gail Gibbons

Little, Brown and Company
Boston   New York   Toronto   London

CATCH THE WIND!
All About Kites

For Maria Modugno

Copyright © 1989 by Gail Gibbons

All rights reserved. No part of this book may
be reproduced in any form or by any electronic or
mechanical means, including information storage
and retrieval systems, without permission in
writing from the publisher, except by a reviewer
who may quote brief passages in a review.

First Paperback Edition

Library of Congress Cataloging-in-Publication Data

Gibbons, Gail.
    Catch the wind! / by Gail Gibbons.
        p.   cm.
    Summary: When two children visit Ike's Kite Shop
they learn about kites and how to fly them.
Includes instructions for building a kite.
    ISBN 0-316-30955-9 (hc)
    ISBN 0-316-30996-6 (pb)
    1. Kites — Juvenile literature. [1. Kites.] I. Title.
                                                                88-28820
TL759.5.G53 1989
629.133′32 — dc 19

10 9 8 7 6 5 4 3 2
WOR
Published simultaneously in Canada
by Little, Brown & Company (Canada) Limited

Printed in the United States of America

Katie and Sam dash up the steps to Ike's Kite Shop. They have finally saved enough money to buy their own kites for today's kite festival.

"Look at all the kites!" says Katie. "We'll never be able to decide which ones to buy."

Ike's Kite Shop is filled from floor to ceiling with square kites, round kites, hand-painted kites — all kinds of kites, in hundreds of shapes and sizes.

As Katie and Sam look around the shop, Ike tells them about kites and kite flying. Any object flown in the air at the end of a line is called a kite, named after the graceful, soaring kite bird.

Historians believe that the Chinese flew the very first kites more than three thousand years ago. At first they made them by stretching silk over bamboo frames; later they covered the frames with paper and decorated the kites with wonderful colors and designs. The Japanese, the Koreans, and the Egyptians were other early kite flyers.

While kites have always been flown for fun, they have also been used for military signaling, in religious festivals, and for science experiments.

In 1752 Benjamin Franklin flew a kite during a thunderstorm to prove that there was electricity in storm clouds. The electricity in the stormy atmosphere struck the line of the kite and traveled down to a brass key tied onto it. It caused a spark and proved to Benjamin Franklin that his theory was correct. This was a dangerous experiment because if Benjamin Franklin had gotten wet, the electricity could have hurt him.

"That's a funny-looking kite," Sam says, pointing to one above his head.

"It's a box kite," Ike explains. "Lawrence Hargrave invented that model in 1893."

Many years ago two brothers named Wilbur and Orville Wright experimented with huge box kites that were strong enough to lift people up into the air. It was experiments like these that enabled the Wright brothers to build and fly the first airplane, at Kitty Hawk in 1903.

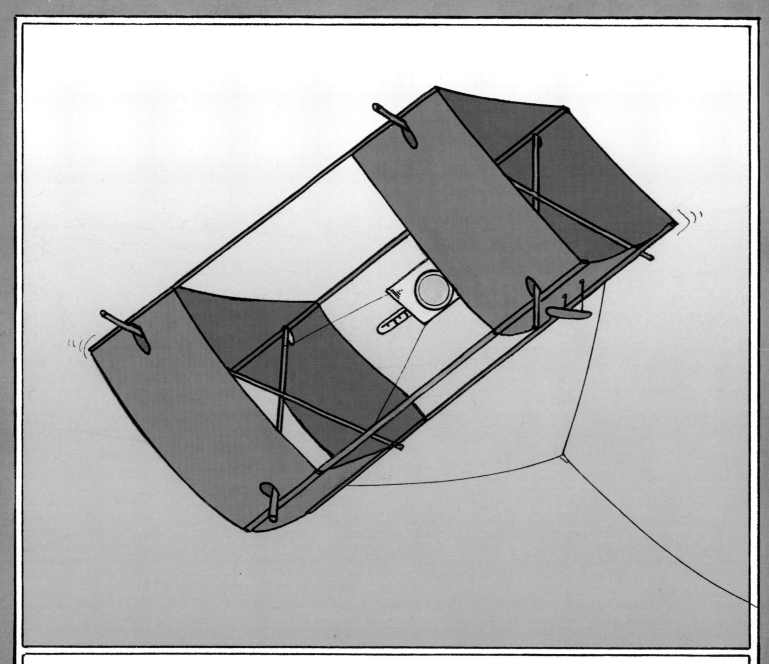

Box kites have even been used to predict the weather. From 1898 to 1933 the National Weather Service maintained kite stations, which flew box kites equipped with thermometers and other weather-measuring devices.

Sam and Katie sort through stacks of kites. Sam finds one that looks like a fish and another that looks like a huge star. Katie holds up one with a clown face painted on it.

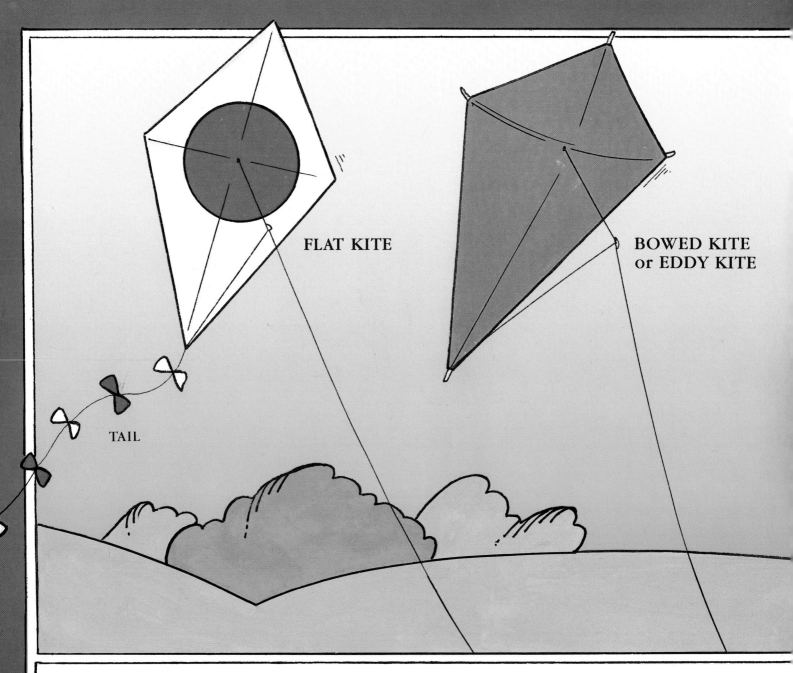

FLAT KITE

BOWED KITE
or EDDY KITE

TAIL

"I didn't know there were so many different kinds of kites," Sam says. Ike explains that most kites follow one of five basic designs. Flat kites need tails to direct them and keep them pointed toward the sky.

Bowed kites don't need tails; their surfaces are curved to create an angle to the wind. This diamond-shaped design was invented by William Eddy, which is why bowed kites are also known as Eddy kites.

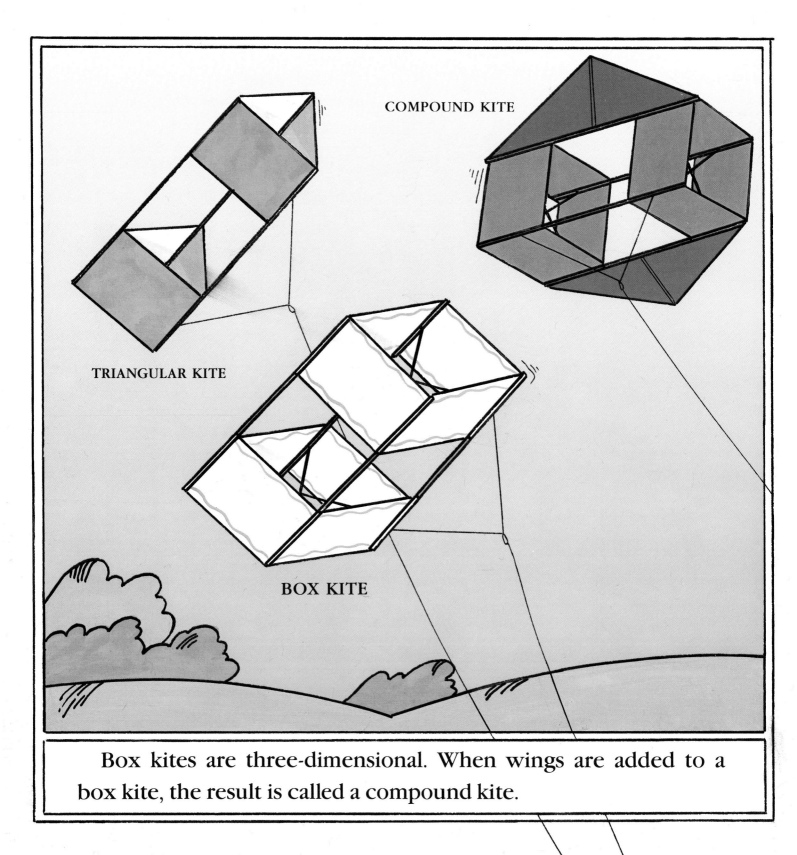

COMPOUND KITE

TRIANGULAR KITE

BOX KITE

Box kites are three-dimensional. When wings are added to a box kite, the result is called a compound kite.

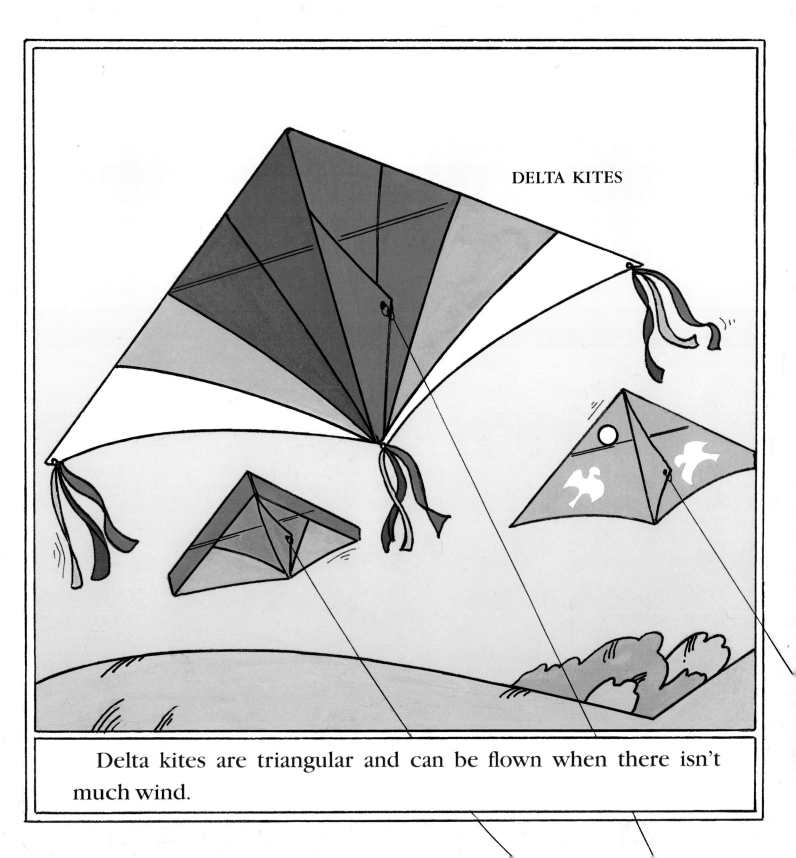

DELTA KITES

Delta kites are triangular and can be flown when there isn't much wind.

FLEXIBLE KITES

SLED KITE

PARACHUTE KITE

Flexible kites are designed to form different shapes when the wind fills them.

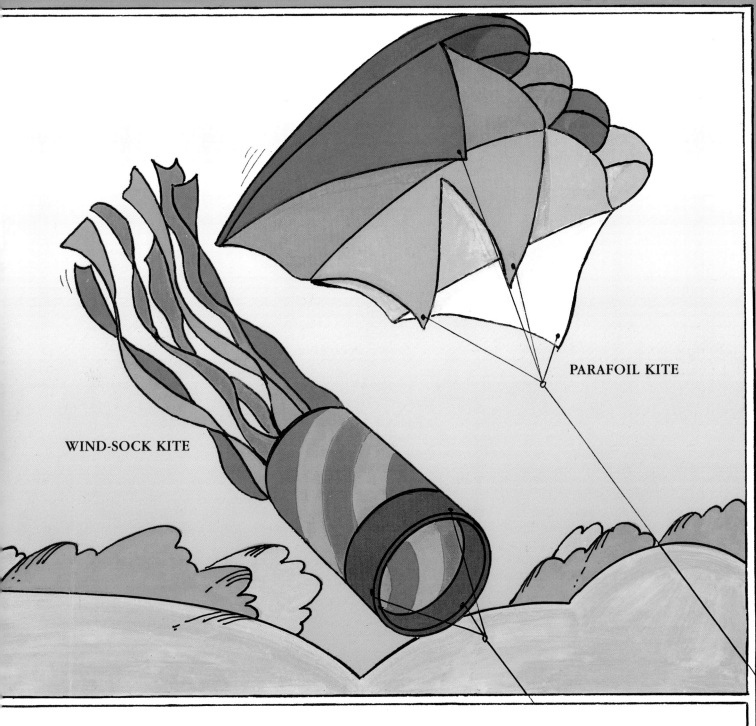

WIND-SOCK KITE

PARAFOIL KITE

They look beautiful when they fly high in the sky.

Ike shows Katie and Sam around his workshop, where he builds many of these kites.

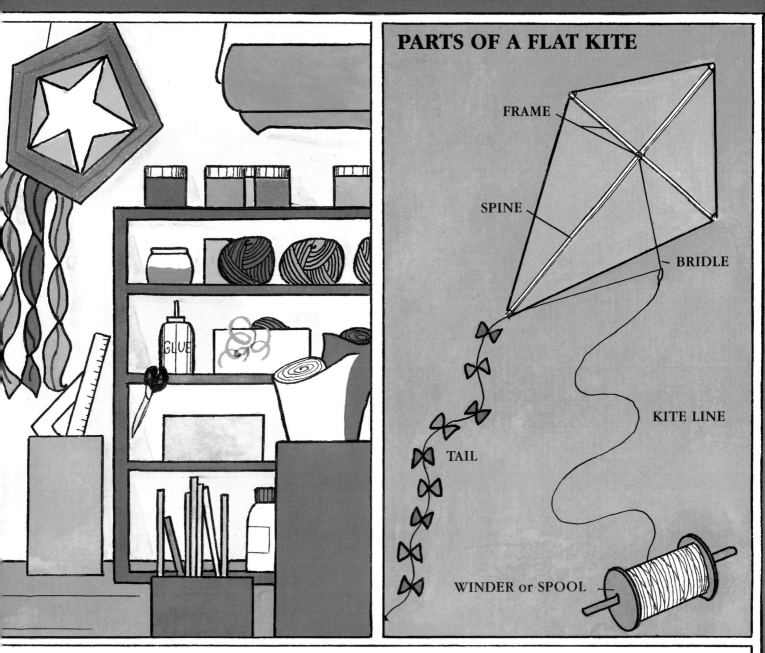

PARTS OF A FLAT KITE

FRAME

SPINE

BRIDLE

KITE LINE

TAIL

WINDER or SPOOL

Kites can be made from many different materials, including paper, cloth, plastic, nylon, and Mylar. Ike's workshop is filled with thin strips of wood, plastic and fiberglass rods, pots of glue, paint and paintbrushes, and tools.

Katie holds up a handmade bowed kite with a cat face on it. "This is the one I want," she says.

"I want this one," Sam says, choosing a delta kite.

They spill their money onto the counter and count up what they owe. Ike ties string to their kites and hands them winders.

"My store is sponsoring the kite festival today," Ike tells them. "I'll be flying a stunt kite. See you there!"

Sam and Katie head for the open meadow where the festival is being held. A wide, open area is the best place to fly a kite. Katie is the first one to see the specks of color high up in the sky.

"Those must be the kites!" she shouts.

The closer they get, the bigger the kites look. Kites are soaring and gliding everywhere. The clear skies and winds from eight to twenty miles an hour make this a perfect day for kite flying. The kites race across the sky, and the crowd looks up to watch them.

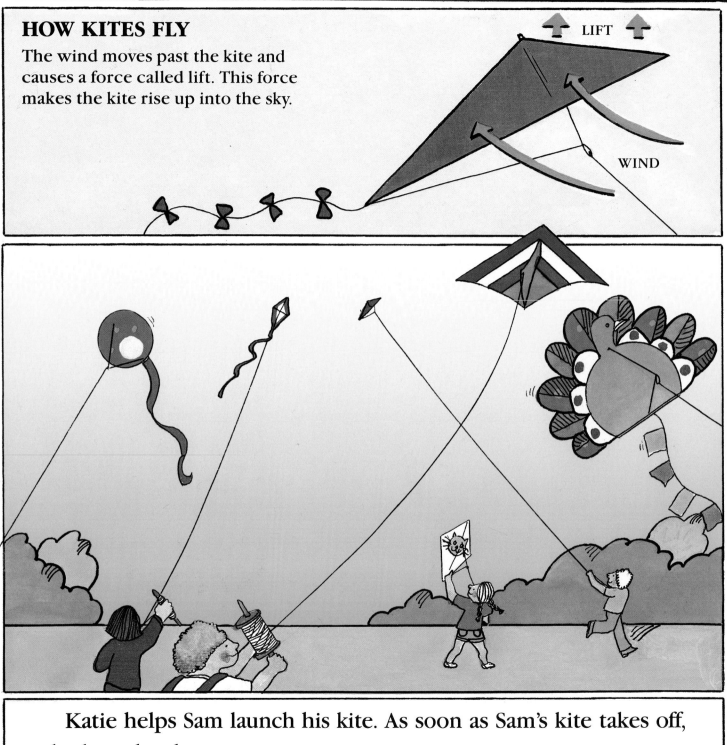

HOW KITES FLY

The wind moves past the kite and causes a force called lift. This force makes the kite rise up into the sky.

LIFT

WIND

Katie helps Sam launch his kite. As soon as Sam's kite takes off, she launches her own.

Up, up, up they go! Soon they are high up in the sky with all the
other kites. Sam and Katie let their lines out further and further.

"Catch the wind!" Ike shouts to Katie and Sam

as he watches their kites join the dance in the sky.

HOW TO MAKE YOUR OWN FLAT KITE

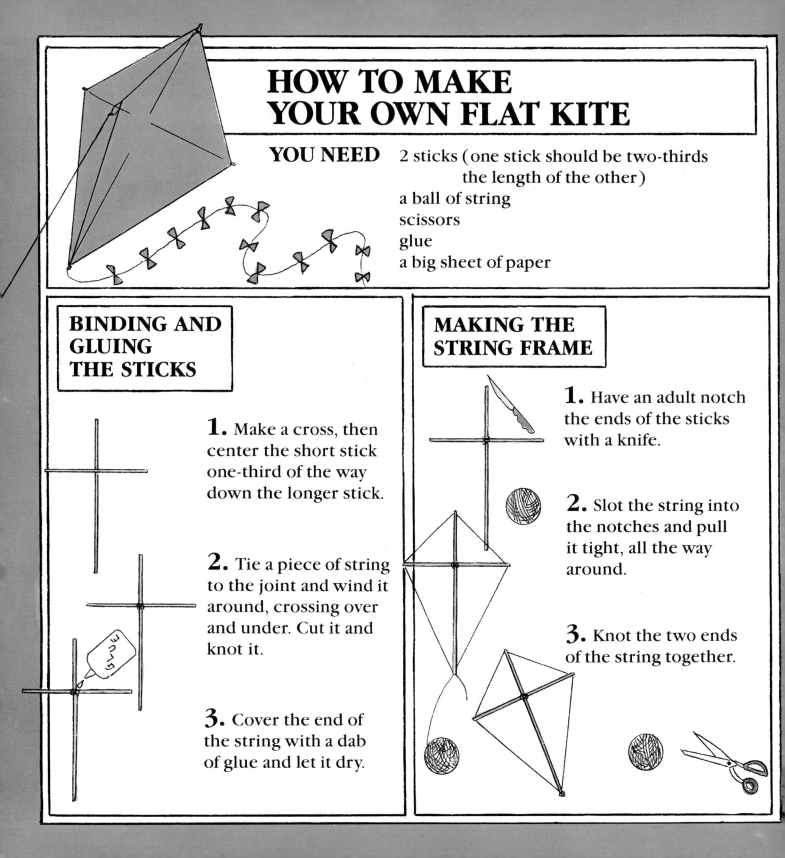

YOU NEED   2 sticks (one stick should be two-thirds the length of the other)
a ball of string
scissors
glue
a big sheet of paper

BINDING AND GLUING THE STICKS

1. Make a cross, then center the short stick one-third of the way down the longer stick.

2. Tie a piece of string to the joint and wind it around, crossing over and under. Cut it and knot it.

3. Cover the end of the string with a dab of glue and let it dry.

MAKING THE STRING FRAME

1. Have an adult notch the ends of the sticks with a knife.

2. Slot the string into the notches and pull it tight, all the way around.

3. Knot the two ends of the string together.

COVERING THE KITE

1. Lay the frame on the paper. Cut all around it, leaving the paper cover a little larger than the frame all the way around.

2. Cut away the corners.

3. Bend the edges of the cover over the string of the frame. Fasten them down with glue.

MAKING THE BRIDLE

1. Cut a piece of string the length of one short plus one long side of the kite.

2. Tie one end of the string around the top of the spine.

3. Make a loop one-third of the way down the string and knot it.

4. Tie the other end of the string to the bottom of the spine. Cut off any extra string.

MAKING THE TAIL

1. Cut a tail string that is five times as long as the kite.

2. Cut a sheet of paper into strips measuring 2 x 3 inches.

3. Tie the strips onto the string, 8 inches apart.

4. Tie one end of the tail to the bottom of the kite.

Now tie the kite line to the loop. The kite is ready to fly!

HOW TO LAUNCH A KITE

BY YOURSELF Stand with your back to the wind. With one hand, hold your kite up in the air, grasping it by its lower corner. With your other hand, hold the winder. When the wind blows, let go of the kite, giving it a little push. Move backward and let out the line.

WITH A FRIEND Have your friend face the wind, holding the kite up in the air in the launching position. Walk backward into the wind, letting out string as you walk. When the wind tugs at the kite, your friend should release it. As the kite goes up, keep walking backward, letting out more line.

HOW TO BRING A KITE DOWN

Walk toward the kite, in the direction the wind is blowing, and reel in the kite line as you walk.

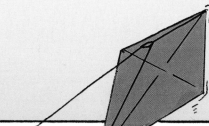

REMEMBER . . .

DON'T fly a kite near electric wires or poles.
DON'T fly a kite in the rain. Electricity will travel along a wet kite line.
DON'T use metal on a kite. Metal attracts electricity.
DON'T fly a kite near the edge of a steep slope.